REFLECTIONS

D0553605

JOHN HENRY NEWMAN

REFLECTIONS
ON GOD AND SELF

EDITED BY
LAWRENCE F. BARMANN, S. J.

HERDER AND HERDER

1965
HERDER AND HERDER NEW YORK
232 Madison Avenue, New York 16, N. Y.

Imprimi Potest: Linus J. Thro
Provincial, Missouri Province
Library of Congress Catalog Card Number: 63-18156
Printed in West Germany by Herder

CONTENTS

INTRODUCTION

In his Spiritual Exercises St. Ignatius Loyola
suggests five steps for a general examination of
conscience. "The first point is to give thanks to
our Lord God for the benefits received. The
second is to ask grace to know and to root out
my sins. The third is to review the time hour by
hour, or period by period, from the moment I rose,
down to the present examination, and to demand
an account of my soul, first of my thoughts, then of
my words, lastly of my actions. . . . The fourth is
to ask pardon of our Lord God for my faults.
The fifth is, with His grace to purpose amendment." In making such an examination of conscience a Christian is reminded of the proper
order and value of things. By thanking God for
His gifts he realizes his relationship to God, the
Creator of all. He humbly expresses the depend-
ence of creaturehood by asking the grace of

self-knowledge. Through the third point any unbalanced or inordinate relationships between himself and other creatures are clarified. Then the Christian acknowledges these disorders which are keeping him from God and expresses sorrow and shame for having allowed their development. With the fifth point comes the determination to amend, with God's grace, the disorders now recognized, and to maintain the divine order in one's life for the future.

Ignatius' daily examination of conscience should be a powerful instrument in the development of anyone's spiritual life. But to succeed in this practice one needs ideas as well as good will.

This little book is a collection of passages from John Henry Newman's sermons. Here are ideas which will help make Ignatius' five-point plan bear fruit in any Christian life. Around the five key themes of Ignatius' examination of conscience are here gathered highlights of Newman's spiritual teaching, the great Christian truths with which we must renew contact – God's transcendence, the meaning of sin, God's salvific love for men, the great possibilities and responsibilities of Christian man, and finally, the peace and joy which, through faith in Jesus Christ, are to be attained in fear and trembling.

The passages in this little book are meant to be read as individual pieces; they should not be read as a consecutive whole. Each selection is proposed as material for reflection and prayer. One passage may be good for one day, another for another. If these thoughts, taken from some of the most celebrated sermons Newman ever preached at St. Mary's, are read in a prayerful, reflective manner, they should begin to bear fruit. St. Ignatius' counsel on self-examination will lead on to the love of God toward which it was intended. And St. Augustine's dictum that to know oneself is to know God should find its justification.

Lawrence F. Barmann, S. J.

THANKSGIVING

I

It would be well if we were in the habit of looking at all we have as God's gift, undeservedly given, and day by day continued to us solely by His mercy. He gave; He may take away. He gave us all we have, life, health, strength, reason, enjoyment, the light of conscience; whatever we have good and holy within us; whatever faith we have; whatever of a renewed will; whatever love towards Him; whatever power over ourselves; whatever prospect of heaven. He gave us relatives, friends, education, training, knowledge, the Bible, the Church. All comes from Him. He gave; He may take away. Did He take away, we should be called on to follow Job's pattern, and be resigned: "The Lord gave, and the Lord hath taken away. Blessed be the name of the Lord." While He continues His blessings, we should follow David and Jacob, by living in constant praise and thanksgiving, and in offering up to Him of His own.

We are not our own, any more than what we possess is our own. We did not make ourselves; we cannot be supreme over ourselves. We cannot be our own masters. We are God's property by creation, by redemption, by regeneration. He has a triple claim upon us. Is it not our happiness thus to view the matter? Is it any happiness, or any comfort, to consider that we *are* our own? It may be thought so by the young and prosperous. These may think it a great thing to have everything, as they suppose, their own way, – to depend on no one, – to have to think of nothing out of sight, – to be without the irksomeness of continual acknowledgment, continual prayer, continual reference of what they do to the will of another. But as time goes on, they, as all men, will find that independence was not made for man – that it is an unnatural state – may do for a while, but will not carry us on safely to the end. No, we are creatures; and, as being such, we have two duties, to be resigned and to be thankful.

Let us then view God's providences towards us more religiously than we have hitherto done. Let us try to gain a truer view of what we are, and where we are, in His kingdom. Let us humbly and reverently attempt to trace His guiding hand in the years which we have hitherto lived. Let us thankfully commemorate the many mercies He has vouchsafed to us in time past, the many sins He has not remembered, the many dangers He has averted, the many prayers He has answered, the many mistakes He has corrected, the many warnings, the many lessons, the much light, the abounding comfort which He has from time to time given. Let us dwell upon times and seasons, times of trouble, times of joy, times of trial, times of refreshment. How did He cherish us as children! How did He guide us in that dangerous time when the mind began to think for itself, and the heart to open to the world! How did He with His sweet discipline restrain our passions, mortify our hopes, calm our fears, enliven our heavinesses, sweeten our desolateness, and strengthen our infirmities! How did He gently guide us toward the straight gate! how did He allure us along His everlasting way, in spite of its strictness, in spite of its loneliness, in spite of the dim twilight in which it lay! He has been all things to us. He has been, as He was to Abraham, Isaac, and Jacob, our God, our shield, and great reward, promising and performing, day by day.

II

Let us thankfully cherish all seasons of peace and joy which are vouchsafed us here below. Let us beware of abusing them, and of resting in them, of forgetting that they *are* special privileges, of neglecting to look out for trouble and trial, as our due and our portion. Trial is our portion here – we must not think it strange when trial comes after peace. Still God mercifully does grant a respite now and then; and perhaps He grants it to us the more, the more careful we are not to abuse it. For all seasons we must thank Him, for time of sorrow and time of joy, time of warfare and time of peace. And the more we thank Him for the one, the more we shall be drawn to thank Him for the other. Each has its own proper fruit, and its own peculiar blessedness. Yet our mortal flesh shrinks from the one, and of itself prefers the other; – it prefers rest to toil, peace to war, joy to sorrow, health to pain and sickness. When then Christ gives us what is pleasant, let us take it as a refreshment by the way, that we may, when God calls, go in the strength of that meat forty days and forty nights unto Horeb, the mount of God. Let us rejoice in Epiphany with trembling, that at Septuagesima we may go into the vineyard with the labourers with cheerfulness, and may sorrow in Lent with thankfulness; let us rejoice now, not as if we have attained, but in hope of attaining. Let us take our present happiness, not as our true rest, but, as what the land of Canaan was to the Israelites, – a type and shadow of it. If we now enjoy God's ordinances, let us not cease to pray that they may prepare us for His presence hereafter. If we enjoy the presence of friends, let them remind us of the communion of saints before His throne. Let us

trust in nothing here, yet draw hope from everything – that at length the Lord may be our
everlasting light, and the days of our mourning
may be ended.

III

Christ has broken the power of the Devil. He
leads us forth on our way, and makes a path
through all difficulties, that we may go forward
towards heaven. Most men, who have delibera-
tely turned their hearts to seek God, must
recollect times when the view of the difficulties
which lay before them, and of their own weakness, nearly made them sink through fear. Then
they were like the children of Israel on the shore
of the Red Sea. How boisterous did the waves
look! and they could not see beyond them; they
seemed taken by their enemies as in a net.
Pharaoh with his horsemen hurried on to reclaim
his runaway slaves; the Israelites sank down in
terror on the sand of the sea-shore; every moment
brought death or captivity nearer to them. Then it

was that Moses said, "Stand still, and see the salvation of God." And in like manner has Christ spoken to us. When our hearts fainted within us, when we said to ourselves, "How is it possible that we should attain heaven?" When we felt how desirable it was to serve God, but felt keenly the power of temptation; when we acknowledged in our hearts that God was holy and most adorable, and obedience to His will most lovely and admirable, and yet recollected instances of our past disobedience, and feared lest all our renewed resolutions to serve Him would be broken and swept away by the old Adam as mercilessly as heretofore, and that Satan would regain us, and yet prayed earnestly to God for His saving help; then He saved us against our fear, surprising us by the strangeness of our salvation. This, I say, many a one must recollect in his own case. It happens to Christians not once, but again and again through life. Troubles are lightened, trials are surmounted, fears disappear. We are enabled to do things above our strength by trusting to Christ; we overcome our most urgent sins, we surrender our most innocent wishes; we conquer ourselves; we make a way through the powers of the world, the flesh, and the devil; the waves divide, and our Lord, the great Captain of our salvation, leads us over.

IV

In every age of the Church, not in the primitive age only, Christians have been tempted to pride themselves on their gifts, or at least to forget that they were gifts, and to take them for granted. Ever have they been tempted to forget their own responsibilities, their having received what they are bound to improve, and the duty of fear and trembling, while improving it. On the other hand, how they ought to behave under a sense of their own privileges, St. Paul points out when he says to the Philippians, "Work out your own salvation with fear and trembling, *for* it is God which worketh in you both to will and to do of His good pleasure." God is in you for righteousness, for sanctification, for redemption, through the Spirit of His Son, and you must use His influences, His operations, not as your own (God forbid!), not as you would use your own mind or your own limbs, irreverently, but as His presence in you. All your knowledge is from Him; all good thoughts are from Him; all power to pray is from Him; your Baptism is from Him; the consecrated elements are from Him; your growth in holiness is from Him. You are not your own, you have been bought with a price, and a mysterious power is working in you. Oh that we felt all this as well as were convinced of it!

V

Oh that we had duly drunk into this spirit of reverence and godly fear! Doubtless we are far above the Jews in our privileges; we are favoured with the news of redemption; we know doctrines, which righteous men of old times earnestly desired to be told, and were not. To us is revealed the Eternal Son, the Onlybegotten of the Father, full of grace and truth. We are branches of the True Vine, which is sprung out of the earth and spread abroad. We have been granted Apostles, Prophets, Evangelists, pastors, and teachers. We celebrate those true Festivals which the Jews possessed only in shadow. For us Christ has died; on us the Spirit has descended. In these respects we are honoured and privileged, oh how far above all ages before He came! Yet our honours are our shame, when we contrast the glory given us with our love of the world, our fear of men, our lightness of mind, our sensuality, our gloomy tempers. What need have we to look with wonder and reverence at those saints of the Old Covenant, who with less advantages yet so far surpassed us; and still more at those of the Christian Church, who both had higher gifts of grace and profited by them! What need have we to humble ourselves; to pray God not to leave us, though we have left Him; to pray Him to give us back what we have lost, to receive a repentant people, to renew in us a right heart and give us a religious will, and to enable us to follow Him perseveringly in His narrow and humbling way.

VI

God beholds thee individually whoever thou art: He calls thee by thy name. He knows what is in thee, all thy own peculiar feelings and thoughts, thy dispositions and likings, thy strength and thy weakness. He views thee in the day of thy rejoicing as well as in the day of thy sorrow. He sympathizes in thy hopes and thy temptations. He interests Himself in all thy anxieties and re- membrances, all the risings and fallings of thy soul. He has numbered all the hairs of thy head; He compasses thee round and bears thee in His arms; He takes thee up and sets thee down. He notes thy countenance, whether smiling or in tears. He looks tenderly upon thy hands and feet. He hears thy voice, the beating of thy heart, and thy very breathing. Thou dost not love thyself better than He loves thee. Thou canst not shrink from pain more than He dislikes thee bearing it;

and if He puts it on thee it is as thou wilt put it on thyself if thy art wise for a greater good hereafter.

.

PETITION

I

It will indeed be a fearful moment when we stand before Him in the sight of men and Angels, to be judged according to our works! It will be fearful for ourselves and for all our friends. Then the day of grace will be over; prayers will not avail then, when the books are opened. Let us then plead for ourselves and for each other while it is called to-day. Let us pray Him, by the merits of His cross and passion, to have mercy on us, to have mercy on all we love, on all the Church; to pardon us, to reveal to us our sins, to give us repentance and amendment of life, to give us present grace, and to bestow on us, according to the riches of His love, future blessedness in His eternal kingdom.

II

Let us then approach God, all of us, confessing that we do not know ourselves; that we are more guilty than we can possibly understand, and can but timidly hope, not confidently determine, that we have true faith. Let us take comfort in our being still in a state of grace, though we have no certain pledge of salvation. Let us beg Him to enlighten us, and comfort us; to forgive us all our sins, teaching us those we do not see, and enabling us to overcome them.

III

Let us aim at, let us reach after and (as it were) catch at the things of the next world. There is a voice within us, which assures us that there is something higher than earth. We cannot analyze, define, contemplate what it is that thus whispers to us. It has no shape or material form. There is that in our hearts which prompts us to religion, and which condemns and chastises sin. And this yearning of our nature is met and sustained, it finds an object to rest upon, when it hears of the existence of an All-powerful, All-gracious Creator. It incites us to a noble faith in what we cannot see.

IV

God grant that we may not attempt to deceive our consciences, and to reconcile together, by some artifice or other, the service of this world and of God! God grant that we may not pervert and dilute His holy Word, put upon it the false interpretations of men, reason ourselves out of its strictness, and reduce religion to an ordinary common-place matter – instead of thinking it what it *is,* a mysterious and supernatural subject, as distinct from anything that lies on the surface of this world, as day is from night and heaven from earth!

V

Now (I repeat) unless we have some just idea of our hearts and of sin, we can have no right idea of a Moral Governor, a Saviour or a Sanctifier, that is, in professing to believe in Them, we shall be using words without attaching distinct meaning to them. Thus self-knowledge is at the root of all real religious knowledge; and it is in vain, – worse than vain, – it is a deceit and mischief, to think to understand the Christian doctrines as a matter of course, merley by being taught by books, or by attending sermons, or by any outward means, however excellent, taken by themselves. For it is in proportion as we search our hearts and understand our own nature, that we understand what is meant by an Infinite Governor and Judge; in proportion as we comprehend the nature of disobedience and our actual sinfulness, that we feel what is the blessing of the removal of sin, redemption, pardon, sanctification which otherwise are mere words. God speaks to us primarily in our hearts. Self-knowledge is the key to the precepts and doctrines of Scripture. The very utmost any outward notices of religion can do, is to startle us and make us turn inward and search our hearts; and then, when we have experienced what it is to read ourselves, we shall profit by the doctrines of the Chruch and the Bible.

VI

He has broken the power of Satan; He has gone "upon the lion and adder, the young lion and the dragon hath He trod under His feet;" and henceforth evil spirits, instead of having power over us, tremble and are affrighted at every true Christian. They know he has that in him which makes him their master; that he may, if he will, laugh them to scorn, and put them to flight. They know this well, and bear it in mind, in all their assaults upon him; sin alone gives them power over him; and their great object is, to make him sin, and therefore to surprise him into sin, knowing they have no other way of overcoming him. They try to scare him by the appearance of danger, and *so* to surprise him; or they approach stealthily and covertly to seduce him, and *so* to surprise him. But except by taking him at unawares, they can do nothing. Therefore let us be, my brethren, "not ignorant of their devices;" and as knowing them, let us watch, fast, and pray, let us keep close under the wings of the Almighty, that He may be our shield and buckler. Let us pray Him to make known to us His will, – to teach us our faults, – to take from us whatever may offend Him, – and to lead us in the way everlasting. . . . let us look upon ourselves as on the Mount with Him – within the veil – hid with Him – not out of Him, or apart from Him, in whose presence alone is life, but with and in Him – learning of His Law with Moses, of His attributes with Elijah, or His counsels with Daniel – learning to repent, learning to confess and to amend – learning His love and His fear – unlearning ourselves, and growing up unto Him who is our Head.

VII

Oh! that we could take that simple view of things as to feel that the *one thing* that lies before us is to please God! What gain is it to please the world, to please the great – nay, even to please those whom we love, compared with this? What gain is it to be applauded, admired, courted, followed, compared with this one aim of not being disobedient to a heavenly vision? What can this world offer comparable with that insight into spiritual things, that keen faith, that heavenly peace, that high sanctity, that everlasting righteousness which they enjoy who in sincerity love and follow our Lord Jesus Christ. Let us beg and pray Him day by day to reveal Himself to our souls more fully, to quicken our senses, to give us sight and hearing, taste and touch of the world to come; so to work within us that we may sincerely say, "Thou shalt guide me with Thy counsel and after that receive me with glory. Whom have I in heaven but Thee. My flesh and my heart faileth, but God is the strength of my heart and my portion forever."

VIII

May He support us all the day long, till the shades lengthen, and the evening comes, and the busy world is hushed, and the fever of life is over, and our work is done! Then in His mercy may He give us a safe lodging, and a holy rest, and peace at the last!

EXAMINATION

I

First of all, self-knowledge does not come as a matter of course; it implies an effort and a work. As well may we suppose, that the knowledge of the language comes by nature, as that acquaintance with our own heart is natural. Now the very effort of steadily reflecting, is itself painful to many men; not to speak of the difficulty of reflecting correctly. To ask ourselves *why* we do this or that, to take account of the principles which govern us, and see whether we act for conscience' sake or from some lower inducement, is painful. We are busy in the world, and what leisure time we have we readily devote to a less severe and wearisome employment.

And then comes in our self-love. We *hope* the best; this saves us the trouble of examining. Self-love answers for our safety. We think it sufficient caution to allow for certain possible unknown faults at the utmost, and to take them *into* the reckoning when we balance our account with our conscience: whereas, if the truth were known to us, we should find we had nothing but debts, and those greater than we can conceive, and ever increasing.

And this favourable judgment of ourselves will especially prevail, if we have the misfortune to have uninterrupted health and high spirits, and domestic comfort. Health of body and mind is a great blessing, if we can bear it; but unless chastened by watching and fasting, it will commonly seduce a man into the notion that he is much better than he really is. Resistance to our acting rightly, whether it proceeds from within or without, tries our principle; but when things go smoothly, and we have but to wish, and we can perform, we cannot tell how far we do or do not act from a sense of duty. When a man's spirits are high, he is pleased with everything; and with himself especially. He can act with vigour and promptness, and he mistakes this mere constitutional energy for strength of faith. He is cheerful and contented; and he mistakes this for Christian peace. And, if happy in his family, he mistakes mere natural affection for Christian benevolence, and the confirmed temper of Christian love. In short, he is in a dream, from which nothing could have saved him except deep humility, and nothing will ordinarily rescue him except sharp affliction.

Other accidental circumstances are frequently causes of a similar selfdeceit. While we remain in retirement from the world, we do not know ourselves; or after any great mercy or trial, which has affected us much, and given a temporary strong impulse to our obedience; or when we are in keen pursuit of some good object, which excites the mind, and for a time deadens it to temptation. Under such circumstances we are ready to think far too well of ourselves. The world is away; or, at least, we are insensible to its seductions; and we mistake our merely temporary tranquillity, or our over-wrought fervour of mind, on the one hand for Christian peace, on the other for Christian zeal. Next we must consider the force of habit.

Conscience at first warns us against sin; but if we disregard it, it soon ceases to upbraid us: and thus sins, once known, in time become secret sins. It seems then (and it is a startling reflection), that the more guilty we are, the less we know it; for the oftener we sin, the less we are distressed at it. I think many of us may, on reflection, recollect instances, in our experience of ourselves, of our gradually forgetting things to be wrong, which once shocked us. Such is the force of habit. By it (for instance) men contrive to allow themselves in various kinds of dishonesty. They bring themselves to affirm what is untrue, or what they are not sure is true, in the course of business. They overreach and cheat; and still more are they likely to fall into low and selfish ways without their observing it, and all the while to continue careful in their attendance on the Christian ordinances, and bear about them a form of religion. Or, again, they will live in self-indulgent habits; eat and drink more than is right; display a needless pomp and splendour in their domestic arrangements, without any misgiving; much less do they think of simplicity of manners and abstinence as Christian duties. Now we cannot suppose they *always* thought their present mode of living to be justifiable, for *others* are still struck with its impropriety; and what others now feel, doubtless they once felt themselves. But such is the force of habit. So again, to take as a third instance, the duty of stated private prayer; at first it is omitted with compunction, but soon with indifference. But it is not the less a sin because we do not feel it to be such. Habit has made it a secret sin.

To the force of habit must be added that of custom. Every age has its own wrong ways; and these have such influence, that good men, from living in the world, are unconsciously misled by them. At one time a fierce persecuting hatred of those who erred in Christian doctrine has prevailed; at another, an odious overestimation of wealth and the means of wealth; at another, an irreligious veneration of the mere intellectual powers; at another, a laxity of morals; at another, disregard of the forms and discipline of the Church. The most religious men, unless they are especially watchful, will feel the sway of the fashion of their age; and suffer from it, as Lot in wicked Sodom, though unconsciously. Yet their ignorance of the mischief does not change the nature of their sin; – sin it still is, only custom makes it *secret* sin.

II

In many, very many ways you may be called upon to bear the ill-usage of the world, or to withstand its attempts to draw you from God; but you must be firm, and you must not be surprised that they should be made. You must consider that it is your very calling to bear and to withstand. This is what you offer to God as a sort of return for His great mercies to you. Did not Christ go through much more for you than you can possibly be called upon to undergo for Him? Did He bear the bitter cross who was sinless, and do you, who are at best so sinful, scruple to bear such poor trials and petty inconveniences?

... I will but call your attention to two points, to which what I have said leads me.

First: Do not be too eager to suppose you are ill-treated for your religion's sake. Make as light of matters as you can. And beware of being severe on those who lead careless lives, or whom you think or know to be ill-treating you. Do not dwell on such matters. Turn your mind away from them. Avoid all gloominess. Be kind and gentle to those who are perverse, and you will very often, please God, gain them over. You should pray for those who lead careless lives, and especially if they are unkind to you. Who knows but God may hear your prayers, and turn their hearts, and bring them over to you? Do everything for them but imitate them and yield to them. This is the true Christian spirit, to be meek and gentle under ill-usage, cheerful under slander, forgiving towards enemies, and silent in the midst of angry tongues.

Secondly, I would say, recollect you cannot do any one thing of all the duties I have been speaking of, without God's help. Any one who attempts to resist the world, or to do other good things by his own strength, will be sure to fall. We *can* do good things, but it is when God gives us power to do them. Therefore we must pray to Him for the power. When we are brought into temptation of any kind, we should lift up our hearts to God. We should say to Him, "Good Lord, deliver us." Our Lord, when He was going away, promised to His disciples a Comforter instead of Himself; that was God the Holy Ghost, who is still among us (though we see Him not), as Christ was with the Apostles. He has come in order to enlighten us, to guide us in the right way, and in the end to bring us to Christ in heaven. And He came down, as His name "Comforter" shows, especially to stand by, and comfort, and strengthen those who are in any trouble, particularly trouble from irreligious men. The disciples, when Christ went, had to go through much trouble, and therefore He comforted them by the coming of the Holy and Eternal Spirit, the Third Person in the Blessed Trinity. "Theses things I have spoken unto you," He says, "that in Me ye might have peace; in the world ye shall have tribulation, but be of good cheer, I have overcome the world." When, then, religious persons are in low spirits, or are any way grieved at the difficulties which the world puts in their way, when they earnestly desire to do their duty, yet feel how weak they are, let them recollect that they are "not their own," but "bought with a price," and the dwelling-places and temples of the All-gracious Spirit.

III

If, then, a person asks how he is to know whether he is dreaming on in the world's slumber, or is really awake and alive unto God, let him first fix his mind upon some one or other of his besetting infirmities. Every one who is at all in the habit of examining himself, must be conscious of such within him. Many men have more than one, all of us have some one or other; and in resisisting and overcoming such, self-denial has its first employment. One man is indolent and fond of amusement, another man is passionate or ill-tempered, another is vain, another has little control over his tongue; others are weak, and cannot resist the ridicule of thoughtless companions; others are tormented with bad passions, of which they are ashamed, yet are overcome. Now let every one consider what his weak point is; in that is his trial. His trial is not in those things which are easy to him, but in that one thing, in those several things, whatever they are, in which to do his duty is against his nature. Never think yourself safe because you do your duty in ninety-nine points; it is the hundredth which is to be the ground of your selfdenial, which must evidence, or rather instance and realize your faith. It is in reference to this you must watch and pray; pray continually for God's grace to help you, and watch with fear and trembling lest you fall. Other men may not know what these weak points of your character are, they may mistake them. But you may know them; you may know them by *their* guesses and hints, and your own observation, and the light of the spirit of God. And oh, that you may have strength to wrestle with them and overcome them! Oh, that you may have the wisdom to care little for the world's religion, or the praise you get from the world, and your agreement with what clever men, or powerful men, or many men, make the standard of religion, compared with the secret consciousness that you are obeying God in little things as well as great, in the hundredth duty as well as in the ninety-nine! Oh, that you may (as it were) sweep the house diligently to discover what you lack of the *full* measure of obedience! for be quite sure, that this apparently small defect will influence your whole spirit and judgment in all things. Be quite sure that your judgment of persons, and of events, and of actions, and of doctrines, and your spirit towards God and men, your faith in the high truths of the Gospel, and your knowledge of your duty, all depend in a strange way on this strict endeavour to observe the whole law, on this self-denial in those little things in which obedience *is* a self-denial. Be not content with a warmth of faith carrying you over many obstacles even in your obedience, forcing you past the fear of men, and the usages of society, and the persuasions of interest; exult not in your experience of God's past mercies, and your assurance of what He has already done for your soul, if you are conscious you have neglected the one thing needful, the "one thing" which "thou lackest," – daily self-denial.

SORROW

I

Let each of us (I say) reflect upon his own most gross and persevering neglect of God at various seasons of his past life. How considerate He has been to us! How did He shield us from temptation! how did He open His will gradually upon us, as we might be able to bear it! how has He done all things well, so that the spiritual work might go on calmly, safely, surely! How did He lead us on, duty by duty, as if step by step upwards, by the easy rounds of that ladder whose top reaches to Heaven? Yet how did we thrust ourselves into temptation! how did we refuse to come to Him that we might have life! how did we daringly sin against light! And what was the consequence? that our work grew beyond our strength; or rather that our strength grew less as our duties increased; till at length we gave up obedience in despair. And yet then He still tarried and was merciful to us; He turned and looked upon us to bring us into repentance; and we for a while were moved. Yet, even then our wayward hearts could not keep up to their own resolves: letting go again the heat which Christ gave them, as if made of stone, and not of living flesh. What could have been done more to His vineyard, that He hath not done in it? "O My people (He seems to say us), what have I done unto thee? and wherein have I wearied thee? testify against Me. I brought thee up out of the land of Egypt, and redeemed thee out of the house of servants; . . . what doth the Lord require of thee, but justice, mercy, and humbleness of mind?" He hath showed us what is good. He has borne and carried us in His bosom, "lest at any time we should dash our foot against a stone." He shed His Holy Spirit upon us that we might love Him. And "*this* is the love of God, that we keep His commandments, and His commandments are not grievous." Why, then, have they been grievous to us? Why have we erred from His ways, and hardened our hearts from His fear? Why do we this day stand ashamed, yea, even confounded, because we bear the reproach of our youth?

If any one who hears me is at present moved by what I have said, and feels the remorse and shame of a bad conscience, and forms any sudden good resolution, let him take heed to follow it up at once by *acting upon* it. I earnestly beseech him so to do. For this reason; – because if he does not, he is beginning a habit of inattention and insensibility. God *moves* us in order to make the beginning of duty *easy*. If we do not attend, He ceases to move us. Any of you, my brethren, who will not take advantage of this considerate providence, if you will not turn to God now with a *warm* heart, you will hereafter be obliged to do so (if you do so at all) *with a cold heart;* – which is much harder. God keep you from this!

II

Let us dare to do His commandments, leaving to Him to bring us through, who has imposed them. Let us risk dangers which cannot in truth be realized, however they threaten, since He has bid us risk them, and will protect us in them. Let us bear, what probably will befall us, the assaults of Satan, the sins of infirmity, the remains of the old Adam, involuntary mistakes, the smarting of our wounds, and the dejection and desolateness ensuing, if it be His will. He has promised to lead us safely heavenward, in spite of all things being against us; He will keep us from all wilful sin: but the infirmities which beset us, our ignorances, waywardnesses, weaknesses, and misconceptions, these He still ordains should try us and humble us, should move in us vexation of spirit and self-abasement, and should bring us day by day to the foot of His Cross for pardon. Let us then compose ourselves, and bear a firm and courageous heart. Let us steel ourselves, not against self-reproach and self-hatred, but against unmanly fear. Let us feel what we really are, – sinners attempting great things, and succeeding at best only so far as to show that we do attempt them. Let us simply obey God's will, whatever may befall; whether it tend to elate us or to depress us, what is that to us? He can turn all things to our eternal good. He can bless and sanctify even our infirmities. He can lovingly chastise us, if we be puffed up, and He can cheer us when we despond. He can and will exalt us the more we afflict ourselves; and we shall afflict ourselves the more, in true humbleness of mind, the more we really obey Him.

III

No true penitent forgets or forgives himself: an unforgiving spirit towards himself is the very price of God's forgiving him. Yet still, though sinners never can be to themselves as if they had not sinned, though they cannot so rid them of their past sins, as to be sure that those sins will not, in the words of Scripture, find them out, and bring retribution upon them; yet, as regards the love of God and of their brethren, in this respect, they are, on their repentance, in the condition of just persons who need no repentance. Let this comfort and encourage all penitents; – they may be high, they may be highest in the kingdom of heaven;

they may be, like St. Paul, not a whit behind the chiefest. Keen indeed must be the discipline which brings them to that lofty seat. Not by languid efforts, not without great and solemn trials is it reached; not without pain and humiliation, and much toil, will they make progress towards it; but it can be gained. This is their great consolation, – it is in their grasp; they have not forfeited, they have but delayed, they have but endangered and made difficult, the prize of their high calling in Christ Jesus. Let them turn to God with a perfect heart; let them beg of Him that grace which wrought so powerfully in the blessed Apostle; let them put on the whole armour of God, that they may be able to withstand in the evil day, and having done all to stand. Let them be sure that, if they have but the will for great things, they have the power. Let them meditate upon the lives of the Saints in times past, and see how much a resolute unflinching will did for them. Let them aim at God's glory; let it be their daily prayer that God may be glorified in them, whether in their life or in their death, whether in their punishment or in their release, in their pain or in their refreshment, in their toil or in their repose, in their honour or in their dishonour, in their lifting up or in their humiliation. Oh, hard it is to say this, and to endure to put one's self into God's hands! Yet He is the faithful God, not willingly afflicting the sons of men, but for their good; not chastising us, but as a loving Father; not tempting us, without making a way to escape; not implanting the thorn in our flesh, save to temper the abundance of His revelations. Whatever be our necessary trial, He will bring us through it – through the deep waters, through the thick darkness – as He guided and guarded the blessed Apostle; till we in turn, whatever be our past sins, shall be able to say, like him "I have fought a good fight, I have finished my course, I have kept the faith; henceforth there is laid up for me a crown of righteousness, which the Lord, the righteous Judge, shall give me at that day."

RESOLUTION

I

I know we shall find it very hard to rouse ourselves, to break the force of habit, to resolve to serve God, and to persevere in doing so. And assuredly we must expect, even at best, and with all our efforts, perhaps backslidings, and certainly much continual imperfection all through our lives, in all we do. But this should create in us a horror of disobedience, not a despair at overcoming ourselves. We are not under the law of nature, but under grace; we are not bid do a thing above our strength, because, though our hearts are naturally weak, we are not left to ourselves. According to the command, so is the gift. God's grace is sufficient for us. Why, then, should we fear? Rather, why should we not make any sacrifice, and give up all that is naturally pleasing to us, rather than that light and truth should have come into the world, yet we not find them? Let us be willing to endure toil and trouble; and should times of comparative quiet be given to us, should for a while temptation be withdrawn, or the Spirit of comfort poured upon us, let us not inconsiderately rest in these accidental blessings. While we thank God for them, let us remember that in its turn the time of labour and fear, and danger and anxiety, will come upon us; and that we must act our part well in it. We live here to struggle and to endure: the time of eternal rest will come hereafter.

II

Let us labour to be really in earnest, and to view things in the way in which God views them. Then it will be but a little thing to give up the world; only an easy thing to reconcile the mind to what at first it shrinks from. Let us turn our mind heavenward; let us set our thoughts on things above, and in His own time God will set our affections there also. All will in time become natural to us, which at present we do but own to be good and true. We shall covet what at present we do but admire. Let the time past suffice us to have followed our own will; let us desire to form part of that glorious company of Apostles and Prophets, of whom we read in Scripture. Let us cast in our lot with them, and desire to be gathered together under their feet. Let us beg of God to employ us; let us try to obtain a spirit of perfect self-surrender to Him, and an indifference to one thing above another in this world, so that we may be ready to follow His call whenever it comes to us. Thus shall we best employ ourselves till His voice is heard, patiently preparing for it by meditation, and looking for Him to perfect what we trust His own grace has begun in us.

There are many persons who proceed a little way in religion, and then stop short. God keep us from choking the good seed, which else would come to perfection! Let us exercise ourselves in those good works, which both reverse the evil that is past, and lay up a good foundation for us in the world to come.

III

What is it your Saviour requires of you, more
than will also be exacted from you by that hard
and evil master, who desires your ruin? Christ
bids you give up the world; but will not, at any
rate, the world soon give up you? Can you keep
it, by being its slave? Will not he, whose creature
of temptation it is, the prince of the world, take
it from you, whatever he at present promises?
What does your Lord require of you, but to look
at all things as they really are, to account them
merely as His instruments, and to believe that good
is good because He wills it, that He can bless as
easily by hard stone as by bread, in the desert as in
the fruitful field, if we have faith in Him who gives us the true bread from heaven? Daniel and his
friends were princes of the royal house of David;
they were "children well-favoured, and skillful
in all wisdom, cunning in knowledge, and under-
standing science;" yet they had faith to refuse
even the literal meat and drink given them, because it was an idol's sacrifice, and God sustained

them without it. For ten days of trial they lived on pulse and water; yet "at the end," says the sacred record, "their countenances appeared fairer and fatter in flesh than all the children which did eat the portion of the king's meat." Doubt not, then, His power to bring you through any difficulties, who gives you the command to encounter them. He has showed you the way; He gave up the home of His mother Mary to "be about His Father's business," and now He but bids you take up after Him the cross which He bore for you, and "fill up what is wanting of His afflictions in your flesh." Be not afraid, – it is but a pang now and then, and a struggle; a covenant with your eyes, and a fasting in the wilderness, some calm habitual watchfulness, and the hearty effort to obey, and all will be well. Be not afraid. He is most gracious, and will bring you on by little and little. He does not show you whither He is leading you; you might be frightened did you see the whole prospect at once. Sufficient for the day is its own evil. Follow His plan; look not on anxiously; look down at your present footing "lest it be turned out of the way," but speculate not about the future.

IV

. . . if it is true that a sinner *may* become a saint, it is at least as true that an innocent person, who has never fallen into gross sin, notwithstanding need not be a saint. It frequently happens that repentant sinners become more holy and pleasing to God than those who have never fallen. There are a multitude of persons who go through life in a safe, uninteresting mediocrity. They have never been exposed to temptation; they are not troubled with violent passions; they have nothing to try them; they have never attempted great things for the glory of God; they have never been thrown upon the world; they live at home in the bosom of their families, or in quiet situations; and in a certain sense they are innocent and upright. They have not profaned their baptismal robe in any remarkable way; they have done nothing to frighten their conscience; they have ever lived

under a sense of religion, and done their immedi-
ate duties respectably. And, when their life is
closed, people cannot help speaking well of them,
as harmless, decent, correct persons, whom it is
impossible to blame, impossible not to regret.
Yet, after all, how different their lives are from
that described as a Christian's life in St. Paul's
Epistles! I do not mean different in regard to
persecutions, wanderings, heroic efforts, and all
that is striking and what is called romantic in
the Apostle's history; but (if I must condense all
I mean in one word) in regard to unselfishness.
All the peculiarity of a Christian consists in his
preferring God and his neighbour to *self*, —
in self-denial for the sake of God and his brethren,
according to St. Paul's words, "None of us
liveth to himself, and no man dieth to himself;
but whether we live, we live unto the Lord, and
whether we die, we die unto the Lord; whether
we live, therefore, or die, we are the Lord's."
But how many there are who live a life of ease
and indolence, as far as they can — or, at least,
who, far from setting the glory of God before

them, as the end of their being, live for themselves, not to God! And what especially lulls
their consciences in so doing, is the circumstance
that they have never sinned grossly; forgetting
that a mirror is by nothing more commonly
dimmed than by the small and gradual accumu-
lations of daily impurities, and that souls may
silently be overspread and choked up with mere
dust, till they reflect back no portion of the
heavenly truths which should possess them. And
thus, while they dream life away, others who
started with them, first, being overtaken by
pride or passion, fall into sin, and lose their way;
and then are shocked and terrified, and manage
to regain it, and run forward impetuously, and
pass by them; and the last become first, and the
first last.

V

Your Saviour calls you from infancy to serve
Him, and has arranged all things well, so that
His service shall be perfect freedom. Blessed
above all men are they who heard His call then,

and served Him day by day, as their strength to obey increased. But further, are you conscious that you have more or less neglected this gracious opportunity, and suffered yourselves to be tormented by Satan? See, He calls you a second time; He calls you by your roused affections once and again, ere He leave you finally. He brings you back for the time (as it were) to a second youth by the urgent pursuations of excited fear, gratitude, love, and hope. He again places you for an instant in that early, unformed state of nature when habit and character were not. He takes you out of yourselves, robbing sin for a season of its in-dwelling hold upon you. Let not those visitings pass away "as the morning cloud and the early dew." Surely, you must still have occasional compunctions of conscience for your neglect of Him. Your sins stare you in the face; your ingratitude to God affects you. Follow on to know the Lord, and to secure His favour by *acting* upon these impulses; by them He pleads with you, as well as by your conscience; they are the instruments of His Spirit, stirring you up to seek your true peace. Nor be surprised, though you obey them, that they die away; they have done their office, and if they die, it is but as blossom changes into the fruit, which is far better. They *must* die. Perhaps you will have to labour in darkness afterwards, out of your Saviour's sight, in the home of your own thoughts, surrounded by sights of this world, and showing forth His praise among those who are cold-hearted. Still be quite sure that resolute, consistent obedience, though unattended with high transport and warm emotion, is far more acceptable to Him than all those passionate longings to live in His sight, which look more like religion to the uninstructed. At the very best these latter are but the graceful beginnings of obedience, graceful and becoming in children, but in grown spiritual men indecorous, as the sports of boyhood would seem in advanced years. Learn to live by faith, which is a calm, deliberate, rational principle, full of peace and comfort, and sees Christ, and rejoices in Him, though sent away from His presence to labour in the world. You will have your reward. He will "see you again, and your heart shall rejoice, and your joy no man taketh from you."

VI

Let us, then, determine with cheerful hearts to sacrifice unto the Lord our God our comforts and pleasures, however innocent, when He calls for them, whether for the purposes of His Church, or in His own inscrutable Providence. Let us lend to Him a few short hours of present ease, and we shall receive our own with abundant usury in the day of His coming. There is a Treasury in heaven stored with such offerings as the natural man abhors; with sighs and tears, wounds and blood, torture and death. The Martyrs first began the contribution, and we all may follow them; all of us, for every suffering, great or little, may, like the widow's mite, be sacrificed in faith to Him who sent it. Christ gave us the words of consecration, when He for an example said, "Thy will be done." Henceforth, as the

Apostle speaks, we may "glory in tribulation," as the seed of future glory.

Meanwhile, let us never forget in all we suffer, that, properly speaking, our own sin is the cause of it, and it is only by Christ's mercy that we are allowed to range ourselves at His side. We who are children of wrath, are made through Him children of grace; and our pains – which are in themselves but foretastes of hell – are changed by the sprinkling of His blood into a preparation for heaven.